Copyright © 2023 Martrell Kelly John

Published by KJ Therapeutic Services LLC
www.kjtherapeuticservices.com

All rights reserved

This publication is designed to provide accurate and authoritative information regarding the subject matter covered. It is sold as a self-help booklet. If expert assistance or counseling is needed, the services of a professional should be sought.

No part of this book may be reproduced or stored in a retrieval system, or transmitted in any form or by any means, electronic, mechanical, photocopying, recording or otherwise, without written permission.

ISBN: 979-8-9888126-0-9

Library of Congress Control Number: TXu 2-378-401

Printed in the United States of America

**Preface**

It has taken me many years to bring this concept to a written format to share with others. I first had this thought shortly after I experienced leaving a career that I had invested so much time, training, and energy. Prior to making a transition into another career opportunity, I experienced what felt like deep depression. In those moments, I reflected on my trajectory like a broken recorder, replaying the story over again and again, only to reach the same ending. I initially never wanted to pursue this career but felt it chose me. After running from this for nearly two years, I succumbed and embarked on a career I could not find listed in the classified section for employment; this career only offered a curriculum at selected number of colleges/universities in other states. Nevertheless, I left my home state of South Carolina, immediate family, and friends. I successfully enrolled into a mortuary program that unfortunately almost closed. To ensure completion of the mortuary classes, I had to abandon my backup plan for job security, i.e., my double major in business management. I remember rushing to attend evening classes while working full-time in the profession and completing my apprenticeship simultaneously. In addition, I sought extra help to achieve adequate skills and constant networking. Since my family did not own a funeral home, I fought hard to overcome the barriers of a male dominated-family oriented industry. All of this was no easy feat! Within a year of becoming fully licensed my job ended ABRUPTLY. I was now facing my worst fear of not being able to find employment in the industry. It was as if I did not belong. There I sat disheartened and asking the same question, "how can this be?"

At the time, I could not name what I was experiencing. I recall a friend sharing with me that I was grieving. Grieving? Hmmm?

Yes, grieving the loss of my first career as a funeral director. I recall pondering this new revelation: Grieving.

HMMM

While finding my way through this maze of uncertainty, one day I wrote the word "COPE" in all caps on a ragged piece of paper.

## Introduction

COPE, a four-letter word we often use saying, "I have to cope better" or "You need to cope better."

What does that really mean? Merriam-Webster dictionary defines it as "to deal with and attempt to overcome problems and difficulties or deal effectively with something difficult."

Truly how does someone cope with everyday life challenges, disappointments, changes, and/or losses? How do you cope with the thoughts, feelings, and changes in perception that are associated?

Loss is another four-letter word that I found can cause a massive upset in an individual's life. Loss comes in many forms: death of a loved one or pet, divorce, severed/conflicted relationships, changes in living arrangements, employment, and physical/mental abilities. It is uninvited and results in an unwanted change. Life looks different than what you anticipated or expected it to be. It requires an adjustment to your sense of being and your perception. Whether the loss/change was anticipated or unanticipated (i.e., considered sudden), it still requires some sort of adjustment.

Ironically, there are other changes in life that perhaps we look forward to such as having a baby, getting married, retiring, going off to school/college, taking a new job, or being drafted into the pros. However, these changes can also result in unanticipated loss and/or changes that require more adjustment than we realize. For example, taking a new job or being drafted to the pros initially presents an opportunity to gain increased experience, more money, an opportunity to pay back loans, and/or public attention (i.e., others to take note of our skills). However, after settling into the new opportunity, many losses can follow. These losses may include loss of privacy, living life based on others' expectations while diminishing your own, loss of passion for the art, and loss of sense of direction, i.e., questioning where I am going in my career. For me, the opportunity brought an enormous learning curb; however, it was time-consuming, and it impinged upon family time and my physical and mental health. Furthermore, I lost confidence in my ability, in myself, and in others. This left a feeling of uncertainty, incredulity, and trust issues. These are just a few of the unanticipated changes and losses. My assumptions about my life were shattered.

So how do we navigate through the challenges? As you deal with the impact of your loss/change, it can be difficult and requires an abundance of emotional, mental, and physical work. As you envision the best approach to face the challenges resulting from an unwanted loss or change, consider this conceptual framework. It is my desire that this mnemonic, utilizing the acronym COPE, will be a self-aid and encourager as you navigate through challenges and losses. Just as it has helped me in many experiences and moments when I felt like giving up, I hope it will provide you with the same. May this become a coping skill to enable you to move with and beyond any loss or change.

# COPE

**C**onfront: It is the courage and willingness to face the pain and challenges that loss/change brings. This is not an easy or comfortable task. Avoidance, whether due to denial, fear, and/or uncertainty, is easier. The thought of facing another day without a loved one and the changes that accompany this loss can feel overwhelming.

The looming question, what will my life look like or how will I make it, haunts you.

ALLOW ONESELF TO CONFRONT

When facing a mental or physical illness, the fear of what this might mean now and as you look to the future collides with reflections of who you used to be. Rediscovering oneself in the context of who I am with a diagnosis, whether physical or psychological, requires confrontation. While all of this can be quite challenging, avoidance only holds you back and delays the inevitable process—learning to live with the changes and finding new meaning, routines, and management.

It takes courage to confront an uninvited/unwanted change. One must first acknowledge that something has occurred. Gaining a deeper and more concrete understanding of the significance of your loss/change is important. Acknowledging and comprehending there are many factors that determine why your loss and change are significant. It helps you to validate yourself when others do not. It allows you to look within yourself with a quality of honesty to confront barriers such as denial or perception of your loss, change, or problem. It helps to identify triggers and understand your thought patterns; to seek ways to tolerate the distress and utilize coping skills to manage it. Seeking an understanding of yourself, the issues, and the whys, provides greater insight into how loss and change impact other areas in your life. It allows increased awareness in identifying your unmet needs and satisfying these needs in an adaptive vs maladaptive manner. Exploring the risks and benefits, pros and cons, you are better equipped to cope with mood swings, anxiety, and suicidal ideations. Recognizing when an intervention is required aids you in avoiding increased levels of distress that exceed your threshold to cope. Though you may feel weak, confronting the inevitable represents a sign of strength.

**for a moment to confront and self-validate:** Ask yourself the question, what am I facing right now that is life-altering? Take a moment to reflect on the changes it has brought to your life as you consider the following factors: the nature of the relationship, level of attachment, benefits from both sides, and how much life differs from the way you wanted or expected it to be. Was this a sudden/anticipated loss/change? What other losses/changes have you encountered as a result? Is this an isolated experience or have you suffered multiple losses/changes previously and what was the timespan? How is this contrary to your beliefs and values and does your culture (i.e., family, organization, society) perceive your loss/change as you do? Look within and ask yourself, what has been my ability to cope with changes/losses in the past? After taking all of this into account, do you understand why your loss/change is significant? If yes or even if the answer is no, sit for a moment and observe your thoughts and feelings about this revelation.

**O**pen: Allowing yourself to respond to and experience the depth of your change/loss uninhibitedly and unapologetically, without guilt and shame. To be able to say, I feel sad, depressed, angry, resentful, confused, or a combination of feelings is liberating. Understanding opposing feelings such as distress yet happiness or not knowing how I should feel, does not only exist but is NORMAL.

When one opens themselves to these feelings, you may feel vulnerable, uncomfortable, or as if you are having "a moment of weakness." Realizing moments of weakness is a natural process of the grief journey. To say to yourself, "I am okay," "I am grieving unapologetically" and/or "I am opening myself up to feel without flight" is a huge step in the direction forward. Acknowledging, that my way of responding to my loss/unwanted change is grief (i.e., my internal response to an unwanted situation, change or loss). Recognizing that grief is not only an emotional response, but also a mental, physical, social, behavioral, and spiritual response can provide relief from the paradigm that keeps you in a perpetual state of constriction. Moreover, my way of mourning is simply my outward expression of what it feels like inside my body and my thoughts about the changes. So, what does this mean? Whatever emotions you feel, you also have thoughts that can be overwhelming. Perhaps you are preoccupied/distracted with thoughts about the changes and loss, and experiencing loss of concentration, anxiousness, confusion, and/or thoughts of hopelessness or negativity.

Physically, you might feel fatigue, insomnia, change in appetite, body aches, and other somatic symptoms. Socially, you may or may not feel the need to isolate or terminate relationships. You may also withdraw from others and/or activities. Behaviorally, you may feel resistance to further change, yearning for things to return to the way they were (familiarity or what felt normal). You may become short-tempered, and experience increased sensitivity, restlessness, or over-activeness. Spiritually, you might find yourself seeking meaning and understanding, questioning yourself, your faith, and/or perhaps your beliefs and the power of prayer. As you can see, every aspect of your life is susceptible to grief.

You might ask the question, why does the intensity vary, and why do I feel so much discomfort? The same factors that determined why your loss and change is significant can define the intensity of your grief response. The intensity can vary based on your shattered assumptions i.e., your perception of your support, differences in the quality of the relationship with your loved one, and/or commitments that are no longer important. Additionally, disruption in such things as finances, stability, routines, traditions, hopes, and dreams can further exacerbate one's grief experience. However, allowing yourself to go through this experience, what can be described as a kaleidoscope of symptoms, and taking note of all these changes (i.e., your mood, physical, social, mental, spiritual, and behavioral) is the start of becoming open. Open to what? Open to the process of self-awareness, which can be empowering during challenges and ongoing changes.

What does this mean? Your eyes become a window into yourself, your needs, and your inner strengths. It enables you to recognize things that cause hurt, more distress, or contrarily that bring comfort. Becoming curious about yourself and asking questions of yourself for a deeper understanding opens the doors to your self-made prison. For example, if feeling intense distress, asking yourself is it my thoughts, people that I am around, or my perception of my situation can lead you to freedom. Curiosity mixed with insight is a catalyst to openness. Freely examining and determining the answers to the whys and how or merely working towards the acceptance of the change and letting go of the whys and how, can reduce susceptibility to depression and isolation. It is wise to incorporate self-compassion as a first step to openness to counter the negative thoughts and feelings of judgement and condemnation that may occur as you seek greater insight into your grief. By gaining this level of insight, you are better positioned to acknowledge and validate your feelings and thoughts about this experience. As you are pressing forward in your journey, you will be more equipped to differentiate the impact of your grief on each aspect of your life.

**and allow for openness/symptom check:** Take a moment to identify your emotional, physical, social, mental, spiritual, and behavioral response. Remember, the same factors that determined the significance of your loss and change can define the intensity of your grief response. Ask yourself, what are my thoughts about this experience? Am I allowing myself to feel and think without judgement and condemnation?

**P**ress Forward: It is becoming accepting of your situation and resisting the urge to change it. It includes self-discovery, executing risks and benefits, and dealing with the consequences of decisions. Additionally, recognizing resiliency, your support system, and self-care, self-assessment, and developing and setting goals—all of this gives momentum to pressing forward. Please know, pressing forward does not mean you never look back.

**PRESSING FORWARD**

As you become more accepting of your loss/change in conjunction with experiencing the intensity of grief that is felt each day, week, month, or year you will press forward. Acceptance equals increased self-awareness and understanding. Reevaluating factors that make your loss/change significant and embracing the roller coaster of grief symptoms that are so strongly felt at random times is relevant to forward movement. Since this is an individualized and unique process, it is imperative to view your experiences through an individualized lens. Be careful not to compare your grief experience or measure your progress to others who have endured similar situations. As you live each day, you are continuously going through changes that will require you to adjust how you view yourself, your thought processes, and the way you once lived life. You will discover that your needs are changing. Quite naturally you will reexamine your life. In reflecting on your life, questions or thoughts may arise. Perhaps unsettling feelings of anger, guilt, or regret may come alive. Replaying events leading up to your initial loss/change and retelling your story is a part of accepting the reality and making sense of your situation. Doing your research regarding your mental or physical illness and educating yourself on what is considered "normal grief" will help you to make sense of your own experiences. Consequently, this helps in recognizing what is and is not in your control, giving you a sense of power and understanding about this present experience. This also provides relief from those unsettling feelings and thoughts.

As you discover yourself and perhaps a new version of you, it may bring mental and emotional twists and turns. At this point, pressing forward is crucial to deterring stagnation. This is a point where you must continue to press forward as it is easy to dwell in the past and become stagnant. Identifying and utilizing techniques to counteract disturbing thoughts is imperative. Such techniques as examining the evidence/facts, questioning what is helpful, necessary, or true, and using the probability scale to determine the likelihood of your worst nightmare and/or consider other outcomes can put you on the path to healing from within.

Therefore, understanding and focusing on your strengths as well as your needs is necessary. Recognizing changes in your support system and letting go of previous assumptions and expectations allows for receptivity of healthier connections, relationships, and support. Find outlets that will bring comfort, reduce anxiety, and increase or stimulate your mood. Understand triggers in your life and learn how to support your way of managing your thoughts, emotions, and responses to self and others in a healthy manner (i.e., distract and self-soothe). Subsequently, have patience, be less critical of yourself and have realistic expectations (i.e., using affirmations, reminders, and coping statements). This is key in pressing forward during the vulnerable and transformable moments. In moving through this process, you will rediscover your purpose, access your strengths, and find you may benefit from the help of a therapist or counselor.

 **to reflect on your needs for pressing forward:** Ask yourself, what are my strengths? How have I changed through this experience? What are my current needs and values? What does my support system look like and how am I supporting my needs? In my goal-setting and forward mindset, where do I see myself or want to gain and tolerate? On my journey towards post-growth, what am I learning about myself? What tools do I need to survive? Always keep in mind, acceptance equals increased self-awareness and understanding. Be mindful of your triggers. In a few weeks, redo your symptom check.

**E**ndure: Maintain commitment to yourself as you are met with challenges and continuous changes. Endurance is required to press forward.

However, it differs because you are working to sustain and hold on to all your beautiful self-discovers, your needs, and your grief experience. Being reminded of the tools to support your needs and focusing on your growth throughout this process is practicing self-care. At times, you may feel that life is unbearable as you encounter others who may irritate you or you find that you are juggling multiple things at an already challenging time. Even disappointments, doubts, and feelings of failure can leave you feeling vulnerable. Believe me there will be vulnerable moments. All of these can create an emotional roller coaster, a kaleidoscope of emotions. One prevalent emotion is sadness most often expressed through crying and can sometimes feel uncontrollable. So, what, allow the tears to flow. Crying is cathartic and a coping technique for the expression of grief. Know that crying and laughter are forms of release.

You may question if any of the techniques are working appropriately. However, understanding that utilizing different techniques may be beneficial until you determine which one works best for you. The goal is commitment to yourself as you endure and press forward. It is imperative for you to balance positive and negative thoughts, feelings, and behaviors, actively engage in self-soothing activities, and intentionally express your emotions. Gauge your emotions at the start of the day and be mindful of signals that alert your senses. Remember that the grief reaction is only temporary, not a setback. Be observant of smaller encounters which include gestures from others or verbal/written expressions that can inspire you. Continue to be your own encourager and magnify your efforts as you press forward.

In this process you are learning to trust yourself and others and rebuild stability. As you continue rediscovering your needs and supports, utilize the techniques that you discovered for soothing and motivating yourself (i.e., laughter—a form of release; positive affirmations; stop-think techniques; leaning on your faith). Be sure to choose activities that encompass all your grief responses i.e., emotional, mental, physical, social, spiritual, and behavioral.

Further commitment to your transformation includes setting new values while understanding that they may change throughout this process. Dwelling on what is out of your control decreases your momentum and increases self-doubt and negative thinking. So, keep pressing forward with endurance and gratitude.

To endure is to hold onto and sustain HOPE.

> *__H__elp – recognizing and accepting whatever presents itself*
>
> *__O__bservant – of yourself, encounters, and environment*
>
> *__P__repare– for whatever lies ahead*
>
> *__E__volve – evaluate progress and celebrate each victory*

**for a moment of reflection on your endurance:** Am I aware of my triggers? What skills have I learned and implemented that meet my needs? Does my toolkit help to self-soothe, bring positive activity, self-care, manage my thoughts, distract, and allow me to let go and accept? Am I redoing my symptom check and noticing differences? Keep in mind, COPE is ongoing, as you encounter a new change or loss you will repeat the process.

In conclusion, this framework is not linear. Each encounter of change requires you to grieve by confronting and becoming open to a new unwanted change, as you validate the significance of your loss. Although loss and change can feel like a domino effect, as you move through this process by pressing forward and enduring, you will rediscover and recreate yourself, a new sense of purpose through growth, and develop a new mindset designed to increase resiliency. It is a forever-changing experience. COPE is here to help you navigate and adapt to your transformation process. Likewise, integrating previous useful and healthy techniques that continue to support your needs is a wide use of your resources. Ultimately, COPE is a resource dedicated to helping you find new meaning and purpose as you come to experience stability and joy in life's moments.

**Epilogue:**

As you have read, my assumption of having a fulfilling career as a licensed funeral director was shattered. It was an unexpected ending to that chapter in my life. However, the cliché "when one door closes another will open" foretold my destiny, albeit a gradual opening as I found my way through the maze of uncertainty. This experience forced me to widen my outlook for increased self-awareness. As I looked deeply within myself and noted my strengths, abilities, and worth, I rebranded my job title based on my coordinating experience i.e., Funeral Service Coordinator. I sought meeting planning as my next step as I thought to myself, hmmm, if I must start over, I should pursue another career. I was fortunate to join a public policy research and consulting firm in Washington, DC. I coordinated meetings to convene high-level policymakers and stakeholders to examine and develop recommendations concerning important health and social service issues for vulnerable populations. The meetings consisted of policymakers on federal, state, and local levels, in other countries or between two countries i.e., United States and United Kingdom. All the while, I continued to take stock of my skill inventory and rediscovered my passion in life which was not just helping others but helping to transition through challenges and changes. Meeting planning would become a transition to my next phase in life. By seeing the contribution of Social Workers as stakeholders in the various meetings, I decided to pursue Social Work as my next career. Ultimately, I would merge my funeral and social worker experience to become a grief and loss specialist. However, through this journey, I utilize every bit of COPE for a strong come back and to get to where I am today, a Licensed Social Worker, speaker, and author. To my readers, stay tuned for my two sequels: changes leading to new opportunities and overcoming a journey of losses. Thank you for this opportunity to share this framework and my story.

**Acknowledgement**  First and foremost, I thank God for sustaining me. I want to take this opportunity to thank my family (including members who are no longer here) and friends for their unconditional love and support throughout life challenges. As I reflect over this journey, there are many individuals who have helped me to bring this concept forth through words of encouragement and/or expertise. From the inception to creation of this booklet, none would be possible without these individuals (listed in chronological order of timing and their role). From the bottom of my heart and on behalf of those who shall benefit, Thank you!

Gwendolyn Cauthen, for first bringing to my attention that I was grieving and supporting me throughout that incredibly challenging time of my life.

Sara Marks-Hairston, known to me as my cousin Melissa, at the start of that dark moment of losing my first career, I received a card along with a miniature card which read "when one door closes, another will open." At the time you were unaware of what I was going through, but simply said "I just was thinking of you and God laid it on my heart to send you this." Thank you for your obedience! I have held this message in my heart throughout as it has helped me to press forward and endure. Still today you will find that tiny card on the first page as you open my bible.

Steven Byrd, my adorable and wise husband, who never let me abandon my idea, but gingerly coached me to the finish line.

Lakia Downs, my mentor and friend in the field of Social Work, thank you for encouraging me to move forward with my idea and affirming I have something valuable to share. I have followed your advice, i.e., "build it out and copyright it for others to utilize."

Brandon Walls, my illustrator who humbly stated "it was an honor" as he worked behind the scenes and chose not to receive any recognition; thank you for helping to construct my concept into visual imagery.

Antoinette "Toni" Sanders, my friend and colleague I first met in Hospice and now serves with in Counseling. You have always been an inspiration and your way of words and deliverance of information is impressive. I thank you for your clinical perspective to help make this simplistic, concise, and understandable for readers.

Nicole Simmons, my cousin/sister, and editor, who played a pivotal role at a significant moment in my life. Words will never be able to thank you for standing in your uncomfortableness to be by my side in the embalming room as I prepared my mother for her last viewing and laid her to rest. You would not leave me!! Thank you for your help then and for sharing your time, wisdom, and gift of editing to help bring this to completion.

Shaneka Jones Cook and Yalanda Glenn, people are placed in a person's life for a reason. We may not understand it in our first encounter, but later, purpose and reasons are revealed. I am grateful for your guidance in the publication of this manuscript. In my heart, I knew this was possible, but you helped pilot this to existence for others to see.

## About the Author

Martrell Kelly John, a native South Carolinian, is a Licensed Social Worker for South Carolina and Maryland, a Certified Grief, and a Clinical Trauma Professional. After moving to Washington DC at age 21, she began her first career as a Funeral Director  which entailed helping families navigate the funeral process and burial. Later she pursued a career in Social Work and obtained her master's from the University of Maryland Baltimore. Thereafter, as an Adoption Social Worker, she worked passionately connecting children to their forever homes while helping both biological and adoptive families adjust to the changes/loss children experience. During a brief hiatus, she had the privilege of serving as her mother's full-time caregiver to ensure the best quality of life in her last year. Martrell would later use her personal experience to help patients peacefully transition, families adjust and move towards acceptance of their loved ones' end-of-life changes, and their bereavement. Trained through the lens of loss merged with personal and professional experience and training, have cultivated a compassionate, diverse, and holistic approach in her current work as a therapist. In addition, her expertise enables her to work with individuals who have experienced traumatic grief and help people of all ages, including children and seniors, grow through challenging experiences.

24

www.ingramcontent.com/pod-product-compliance
Lightning Source LLC
Chambersburg PA
CBHW070052070426
42449CB00012BA/3239